CONTENTS PAGE

NUMBER INDEX

PICTURE INDEX

WORD INDEX
CONSONANTS

WORD INDEX
VOWELS

PHONEME SONGS
Consonants 01-24
Vowels 25-44

Theme Song 45

Information Page

PLAY the vocal and instrumental soundtracks to learn
the words for the 45 songs in this colourful 96-page book.

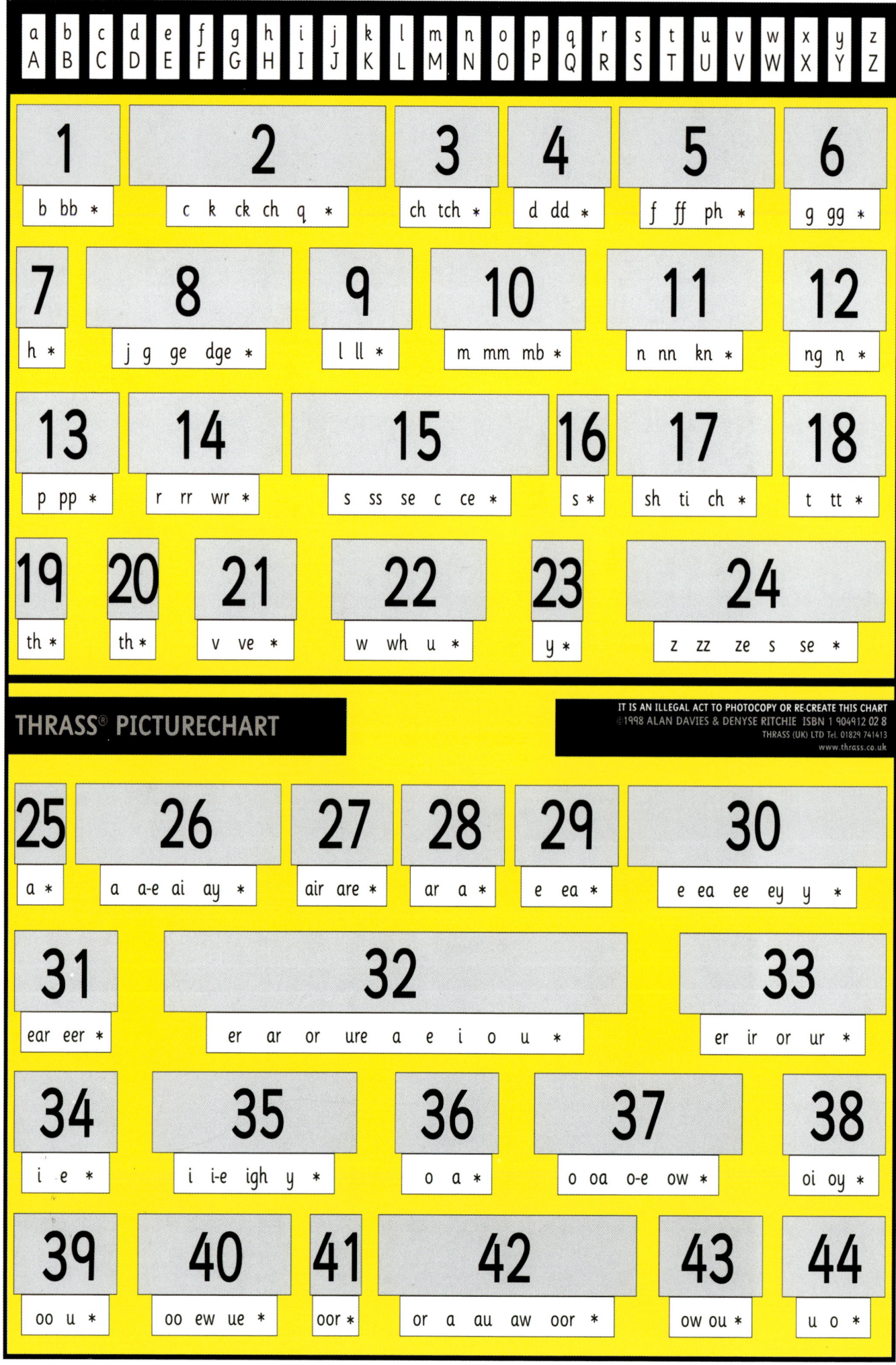

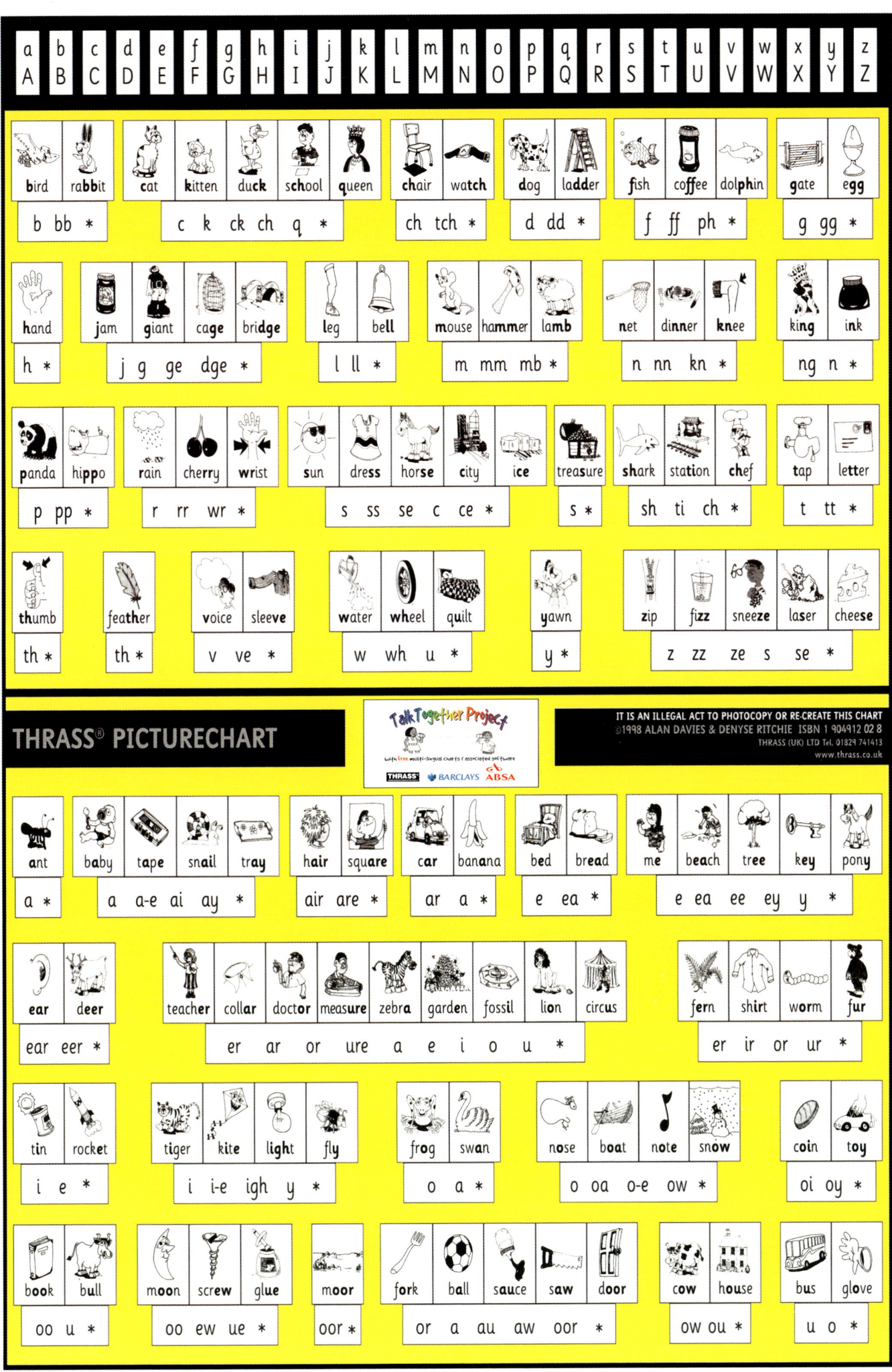

01	Fly little bird	b bb	Hip Hop
02	Rock and roll jive	c k ck ch q	Jive
03	Been sitting on my chair	ch tch	60's 8 beat
04	My dog Spot	d dd	70's Disco
05	I am a fish	f ff ph	Reggae
06	My crazy Granny	g gg	Country Waltz
07	Give me a high five	h	Bubblegum Pop
08	Please eat some jam, Giant	j g ge dge	Dixieland
09	Ring the bell	l ll	Celtic Dance
10	Bruce the Mouse	m mm mb	Country Shuffle
11	I'm gonna take my net	n nn kn	Soul
12	Bring me my pen	ng n	Baroque Concerto
13	You don't get pandas in Africa	p pp	African Round
14	I can't go out to play today	r rr wr	Twist
15	Saw you in the sun	s ss se c ce	Hard Rock
16	Treasure have I	s	Oriental Pop
17	A scary man	sh ti ch	Secret Service
18	Drip, drip, tap	t tt	Swing
19	Abantwana be Africa	th	African
20	Beautiful feather	th	Guitar Serenade
21	Children of the World	v ve	Broadway Ballad
22	My Chihuahua is a thirsty fella	w wh u	Mexican Dance
23	Yawn in the morning	y	Sirtaki
24	It's cold today	z zz ze s se	Big Band

25	My name is Jean Pierre	a	French Musette
26	The music was so loud	a a-e ai ay	Swinging Boogie
27	Disco hair	air are	80's Disco
28	A great big gorilla	ar a	Charleston
29	Get outta bed	e ea	Hoedown
30	Just me on the beach	e ea ee ey y	Hawaiian
31	The oom pah pah melody	ear eer	Ober Waltz
32	I had a teacher	er ar or ure	
		a e i o u	Bluegrass
33	My teddy bear and I	er ir or ur	Typical 6/8
34	Tin Can Man	i e	Sci-fi March
35	There is a bright shining tiger	i i-e igh y	Pentatonic
36	Once upon a time	o a	Viennese Waltz
37	Eskimos kiss with their nose	o oa o-e ow	Jazz Ballad
38	My coin	oi oy	Blues
39	I am reading a book	oo u	Pasodoble
40	The moon fell out of the sky	oo ew ue	Ragtime
41	I'm a Scottish dragon	oor	Highland Waltz
42	At six o'clock	or a au	
		aw oor	Fun 4/4
43	Do you know I have a cow?	ow ou	Irish Dance
44	Riding along in the bus with 'u'	u o	Orchestra Polka

THEME SONG

45	THRASS SING-A-LONG CD Song	'a' 'b' 'c'	Fantasy

Fly little bird

Fly, fly, fly, fly little **bird**;

Hip, hip, hop, hip, hop **rabbit**. [x 4]

Spell it, yeah; spell it, yeah,

Bird with 'b', ra**bb**it with double 'b'.

Spell it, yeah; spell it, yeah,

Bird with 'b', ra**bb**it with double 'b'. [P1] [P2]

Yeah!

NOT PHOTOCOPIABLE © 2007 ALARY LTD

Phoneme Symbol = b   Musical Style: Hip Hop

Rock and roll jive

02

We'll do the **cat**, **kitten**, **duck**, **school**

Rock and roll jive. [x 2]

Cat is 'c', **k**itten is 'k', du**ck** is 'c' 'k',

S**ch**ool is 'c' and 'h',

And don't forget the **queen**, **queen**,

Her Majesty the **queen**, **queen**.

Queen is spelt with 'q', **q**ueen,

Her Majesty the **queen**, **queen**. [P1] [P2]

A boom, boom, boom, boom, boom!

NOT PHOTOCOPIABLE © 2007 ALARY LTD

Phoneme Symbol = k

Musical Style: Jive

Been sitting on my chair

Been sitting on my **chair**,
Waiting for the bell to ring.
(echo) Let the bell ring; please let the bell ring.
Been looking at my **watch**,
'Cause I wanna go and sing,
(echo) Go and sing, wanna go and sing.

I sing about letters out in the sun,
Like 'c' and 'h' in **ch**air.
Use 't' 'c' 'h' for wa**tch**, everyone.
Lovely letters everywhere. [S]

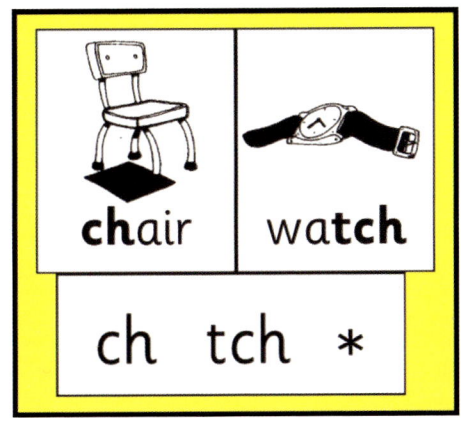

NOT PHOTOCOPIABLE © 2007 ALARY LTD

Phoneme Symbol = tʃ   Musical Style: 60's 8 beat

My dog Spot

My **dog** Spot, he can do a lot of tricks.

My **dog** Spot, he can run and fetch a stick.

My **dog** Spot climbs a **ladder** to the top,

To the top, my **dog** Spot.

Now la**dd**er has two 'd's and **d**og has one;

La**dd**er has two 'd's and **d**og has one.

La**dd**er has two 'd's and **d**og has one.

(spoken) Now where has Spot

The clever **dog** gone? [S] [P1]

Phoneme Symbol = d   Musical Style: 70's Disco

ff ph f

I am a fish

I am a **fish** and my name is Sam.

I come from the islands Caribbean.

I swim all day in the deep blue sea

And drink **coffee** with my **dolphin** buddy.

Now **f**ish is one 'f' and co**ff**ee is two,

And dol**ph**in is 'p' 'h', you know it's true.

Now **f**ish is one 'f' and co**ff**ee is two,

And dol**ph**in is 'p' 'h', you know it's true. [P1]

NOT PHOTOCOPIABLE © 2007 ALARY LTD

Phoneme Symbol = f

Musical Style: Reggae

My crazy granny

My crazy Granny jumped over the **gate**,

And I held the pie that we made for the fete.

I helped her to mix it. I put in one **egg**.

Be careful dear Granny

Or you'll break your leg.

Jump over the **g**ate and spell it with 'g'.

Jump over the **g**ate and spell it with 'g'.

Now e**gg** has double 'g'.

Please spell it with me.

Now e**gg** has double 'g'.

Please spell it with me. [P1]

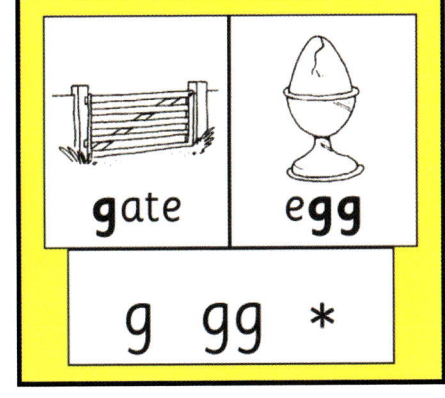

NOT PHOTOCOPIABLE © 2007 ALARY LTD

Phoneme Symbol = g   Musical Style: Country Waltz

Give me a high five

Give me a high five with your **hand**. [x 3]
A high five with your **hand**.

Give me a low five with your **hand**. [x 3]
A low five with your **hand**.

Now let us spell **h**and with one 'h'. [x 3]
Spell **h**and with one 'h'.

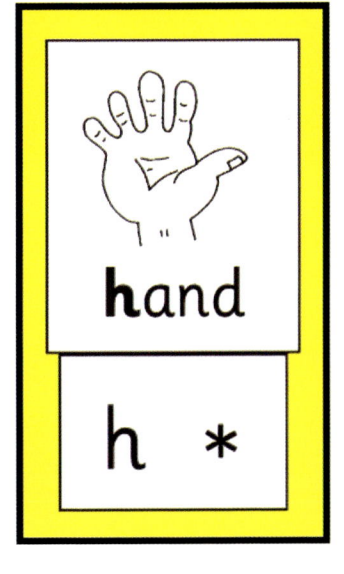

NOT PHOTOCOPIABLE © 2007 ALARY LTD

Phoneme Symbol = h   Musical Style: Bubblegum Pop

Please eat some jam, Giant

Please eat some **jam**, **G**iant.

Don't you cry,

For out of its **cage** your bird did fly

Over the **bridge** and far away.

Oh dear **g**iant, you need cheering up today.

Children, spell **j**am with just one 'j',

Giant is easy, use only one 'g'.

Ca**ge** is a digraph. It's 'g' and 'e'.

Bri**dge** is a trigraph. It's 'd', 'g', 'e'. [P1]

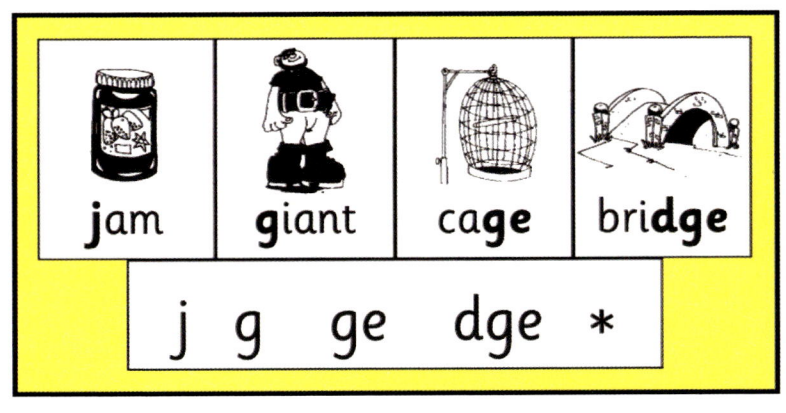

Phoneme Symbol = ʤ   Musical Style: Dixieland

Ring the bell

Kick your right **leg**, kick your left **leg**,

Clap your hands and ring the **bell**.

Bend your right **leg**, bend your left **leg**,

Clap your hands and ring the **bell**.

Shake your right **leg**, shake your left **leg**,

Clap your hands and ring the **bell**.

Stamp your right **leg**, stamp your left **leg**,

Clap your hands and ring the **bell**.

Bell has double ‘l’, leg has one ‘l’,

Ring the **bell**. Let’s hear you spell. [x 4] [S]

Category
THRASS®
TEACHING HANDWRITING READING AND SPELLING SKILLS
FAMILY SING-A-LONG

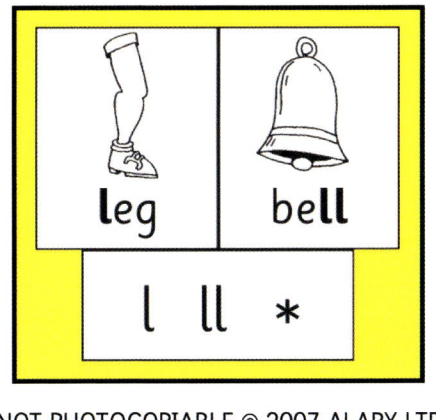

Phoneme Symbol = l

Musical Style: Celtic Dance

Bruce the Mouse

I come from Australia

And my name is Bruce the **Mouse**.

I'm a handyman and with my **hammer** I built my house.

I help my friends, when their things need fixing,

Like Farmer Tom's fence when his **lamb** went missing.

If you come Down Under, please visit Bruce the **Mouse**,

And we'll have tea by the billabong,

'Cause that's where you'll find

Bruce the **Mouse** and his house.

Mouse has one 'm', ha**mm**er has two, [x 3]

And that little lost la**mb** is spelt with 'm' and 'b'.

Please let us know if that **lamb** you see.

Phoneme Symbol = m   Musical Style: Country Shuffle

I'm gonna take my net

I'm gonna take my **net** and catch my **dinner**,
Bended on one **knee**. [x 3]
Just hope that little tasty fish
Don't get away from me.

I'm gonna spell my words with lovely letters,
Like **n**et with one 'n'.
I'm gonna spell my words with lovely letters,
Like di**nn**er with double 'n'.
I'm gonna spell my words with lovely letters,
Like **kn**ee with 'k' and 'n'.
This soulful song is so much fun,
I wanna sing it again. [P1]

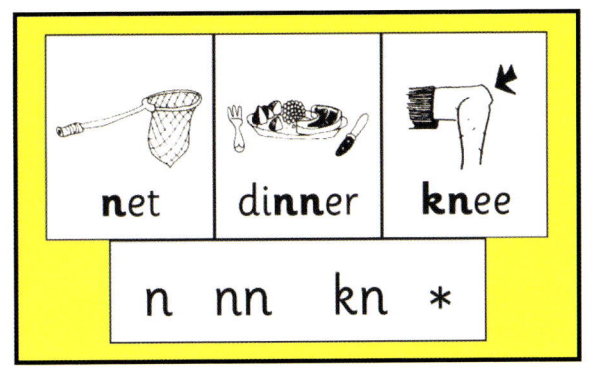

Phoneme Symbol = n   Musical Style: Soul

Bring me my pen

"I need to write some letters", said the **king**.

"Bring me my pen and bring me some **ink**".

"I need to write some letters", said the **king**.

"Bring me my pen and bring me **ink**".

"How do I spell ki**ng**?" said the **king**,

"Your Majesty, use 'n' and 'g' ".

"How do I spell i**n**k?" said the **king**,

"Your Majesty, use one 'n' ". [S]

Phoneme Symbol = ŋ   Musical Style: Baroque Concerto

You don't get pandas in Africa

You don't get **pandas** in Africa,

Only a **hippo** or two.

You don't get **pandas** in Africa,

Only a **hippo** or two.

Panda has one 'p', hi**pp**o has two.

Panda has one 'p', hi**pp**o has two.

Panda has one 'p', hi**pp**o has two.

Panda has one 'p', hi**pp**o has two. [P1+P2]

Phoneme Symbol = p   Musical Style: African Round

I can't go out to play today

I can't go out to play today,

Because the **rain** won't go away.

I think I'll bake a **cherry** cake,

And, for my **wrist**, a bracelet make.

Rain has one 'r', che**rr**y has two,

'W' plus 'r' is **wr**ist. Let's twist.

Rain has one 'r', che**rr**y has two,

'W' plus 'r' is **wr**ist. Let's twist. [S]

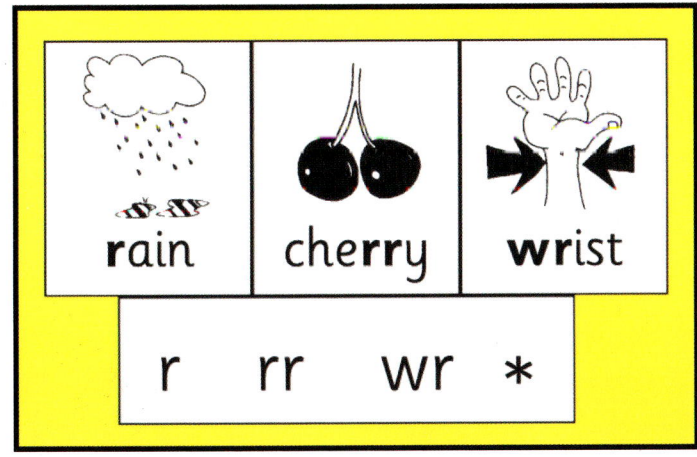

Phoneme Symbol = r   Musical Style: Twist

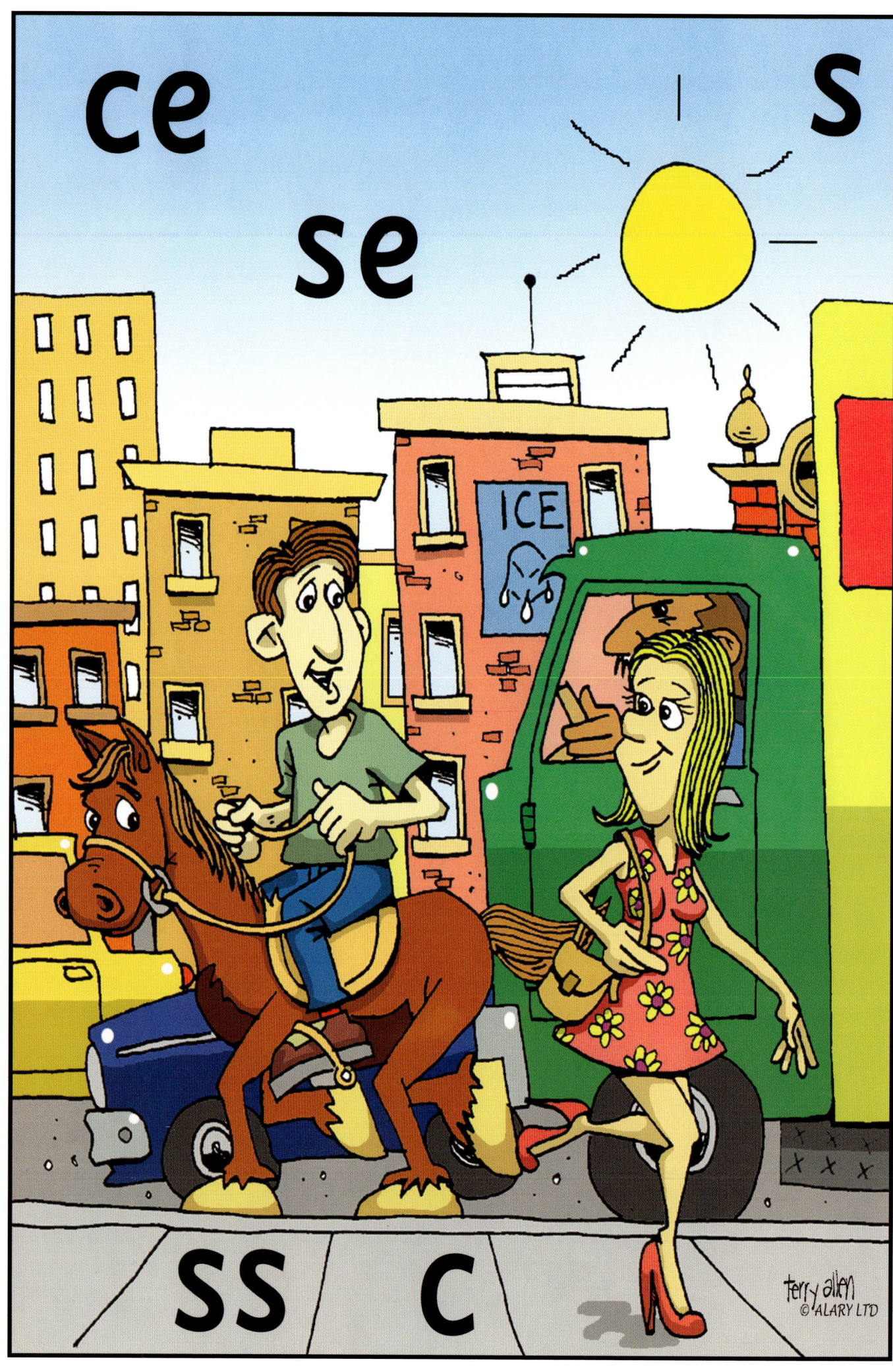

Saw you in the sun

Saw you in the **sun** in your pretty **dress**,

While riding my **horse** in the **city**.

Saw you in the **sun** in your pretty **dress**,

While riding my **horse** in the **city**.

Need some **ice**, 'cause it's so hot,

'Cause that **sun** beats down a lot. [P1]

Sun has 's' and dre**ss** 's' 's',

Hor**se** 's' 'e' and **c**ity has 'c',

Ice, 'c' 'e', i**ce**, 'c' 'e', i**ce**, 'c' 'e'! [P1] [P2]

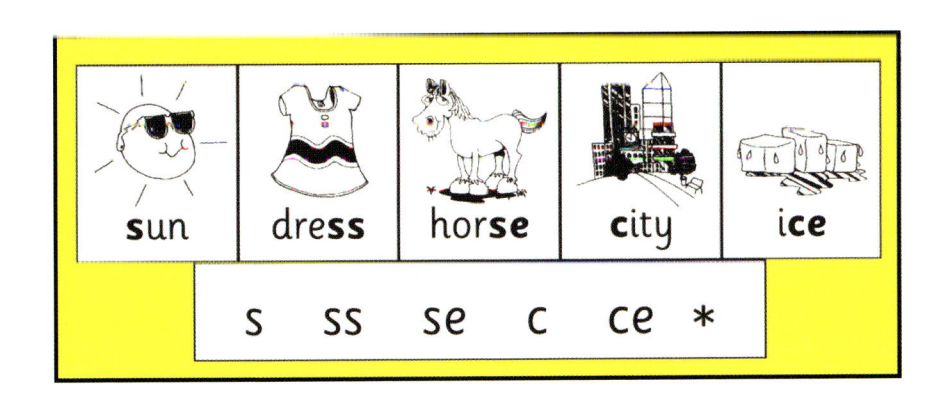

Phoneme Symbol = S

Musical Style: Hard Rock

S

Treasure have I

Tre**a**s**u**r**e** have I, in a secret place,

Diamonds and pearls, in a wooden case.

If you need to spell trea**s**ure,

You must use one 's'.

If you need to spell trea**s**ure,

You must use one 's'. [S]

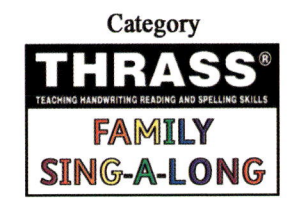

Phoneme Symbol = 3   Musical Style: Oriental Pop

sh ch ti

A scary man

A scary man with a **shark** tattoo
Walks through the **station** and stares at you.
You've seen him before
And you think he's a spy,
But he's disguised as a **chef**
And you just don't know why!

The scary man with the **shark** tattoo,
Says "**Sh**ark is 's' 'h' ", reminding you.
It's not a lie that sta**ti**on's 't' 'i',
And **ch**ef is 'c' and 'h'
But I just don't know why.

Phoneme Symbol = ∫   Musical Style: Secret Service

tt   t

Drip, drip, tap

Drip, drip, **tap**,
Drip, drip, **tap**,
That **tap** keeps dripping all day.
Gonna write a **letter** to my friend the plumber,
And ask him to fix that dripping right away.

Drip, drip, **tap**,
Drip, drip, **tap**,
That **tap** is spelt with one 't',
Gonna write a **letter** to my friend the plumber,
And when I write,
I will spell le**tt**er double 't'. [P1]

NOT PHOTOCOPIABLE © 2007 ALARY LTD

Phoneme Symbol = t

Musical Style: Swing

th

Abantwana be Africa

Hey! Put your **thumbs** up,
'Cause you are okay.

Spell **th**umb with 't' and 'h',
And say, "Hey, I'm okay".
Abantwana be Africa,
Abantwana be Africa,
Abantwana be Africa,
Abantwana be Africa.*

Let all the children everywhere
Join Africa, put your **thumbs** in the air
And say, "Hey! We're okay".

* Zulu for 'Children of Africa'

Phoneme Symbol = θ

Musical Style: African

th

Beautiful feather

Beautiful **feather**, float on the breeze,

Over the roof tops, over the trees.

Beautiful **feather**, soft and light,

I'll spell you with 't' 'h'

When fea**th**er I write.

Beautiful **feather**, float on the breeze,

Over the roof tops, over the trees.

Beautiful **feather**, soft and light,

I'll spell you with 't' 'h'

When fea**th**er I write.

Category
THRASS
FAMILY SING-A-LONG

feather
th *

NOT PHOTOCOPIABLE © 2007 ALARY LTD

Phoneme Symbol = ð   Musical Style: Guitar Serenade

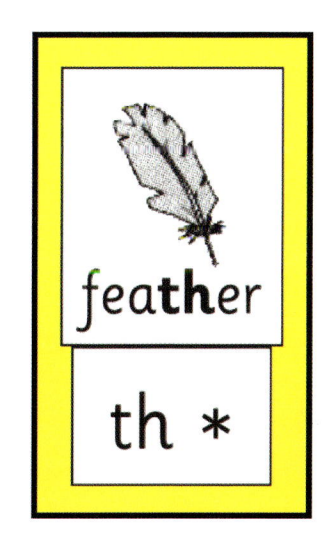

v ve

Learn your letters...

Children of the World

Children of the World, let your **voices** sing.

Wear your heart on your **sleeve**, let your emotions ring.

Children of the World, let your **voices** sing,

You are the future of tomorrow, so let your **voices** sing.

Lift your **voices**, lift your **voices** and sing;

Lift your **voices**, lift your **voices** and sing.

Children of the World, let your **voices** sing.

Learn your letters. Remember that **v**oice has one 'v'.

Children of the world, let your **voices** sing.

Learn your letters. Remember that slee**ve** has 'v' and 'e'.

[P2]

Phoneme Symbol = V   Musical Style: Broadway Ballad

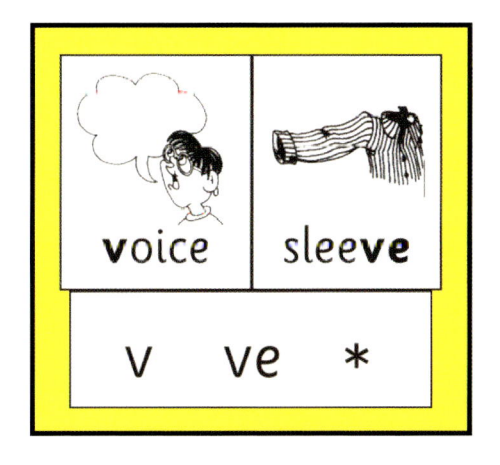

u wh

w

My Chihuahua is a thirsty fella

My Chihuahua is a thirsty fella.
He drinks ten litres of **water**.
My Chihuahua is a thirsty fella.
He drinks ten litres of **water**.

He chases the **wh**eel going round and round.
His bark, it is such a strange squeaky sound.
[P1]

A patchwork **qu**ilt is his favourite bed.
It is blue and yellow and green and red. [P1]

Spell **w**ater with 'w' and q**u**ilt with 'u',
'W' and 'h' for **wh**eel, it's true. [P1]

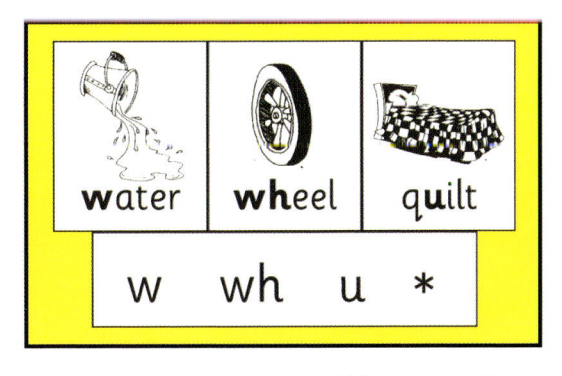

Phoneme Symbol = w   Musical Style: Mexican Dance

y

Yawn in the morning

Yawn in the morning,

Yawn in the evening.

Yawn is spelt with one 'y'. [x 2]

Yawn in the morning,

Yawn in the evening.

Yawn is spelt with one 'y'. [x 2]

Yawn in the morning,

Yawn in the evening.

Yawn is spelt with one 'y'.

[x 2]

Category
THRASS®
TEACHING HANDWRITING READING AND SPELLING SKILLS
FAMILY SING-A-LONG

yawn

y *

NOT PHOTOCOPIABLE © 2007 ALARY LTD

Phoneme Symbol = **j**   Musical Style: Sirtaki

ze zz z
se   s

It's cold today

It's cold today,

So I **zip** up my jacket so I don't get the flu,

But I think it's too late, 'cause

I'm already feelin' kinda blue.

My mum gets all upset and in a tizz.

She gives me yukky medicine that goes **fizz**!

She says that it will stop my **sneeze**,

But it's red like a **laser**

And smells like **cheese**!

Now **z**ip is 'z' and fi**zz** 'z' 'z'.

I really think that I should go lie in bed.

Snee**ze** has 'z' and 'e',

La**s**er has one 's' and chee**se** 's' 'e'.

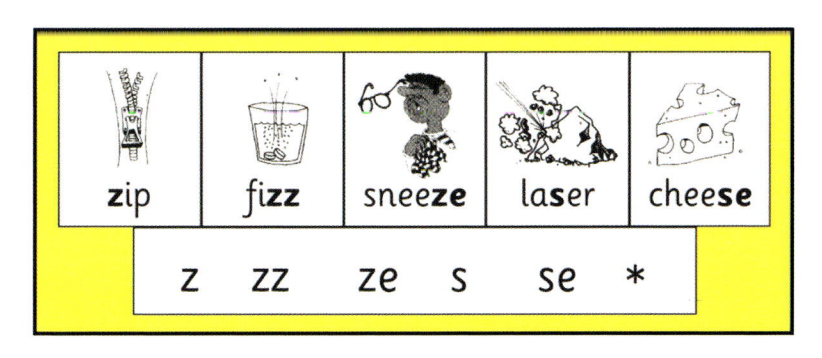

Phoneme Symbol = Z

Musical Style: Big Band

a

My name is Jean Pierre

My name is Jean Pierre.

I live on the Champs-Élysées.

I'm the bravest **ant** that ever lived,

In the city of love, Paris.

If you are spelling **a**nt,

Remember to use one 'a'

And then think of me there,

Brave **ant**, Jean Pierre,

In the city of love, Paris. [S]

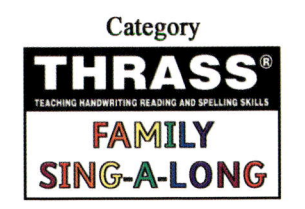

Phoneme Symbol = æ   Musical Style: French Musette

ay   a-e
   a
ai

The music was so loud

The music was so loud, it made my **baby** cry.
It was a **tape** about a little **snail** with funny eyes.
I brought in a **tray**, with a cake I baked today.
It helped poor **baby** wipe those little tears away.
I brought in a **tray**, with a cake I baked today.
It helped poor **baby** wipe those little tears away.

B**a**by 'a', t**a**p**e** 'a' and 'e',
Sn**ai**l 'a' and 'i', tr**ay** 'a' 'y',
Tr**ay** 'a' 'y', tr**ay** 'a' 'y'. [P1]

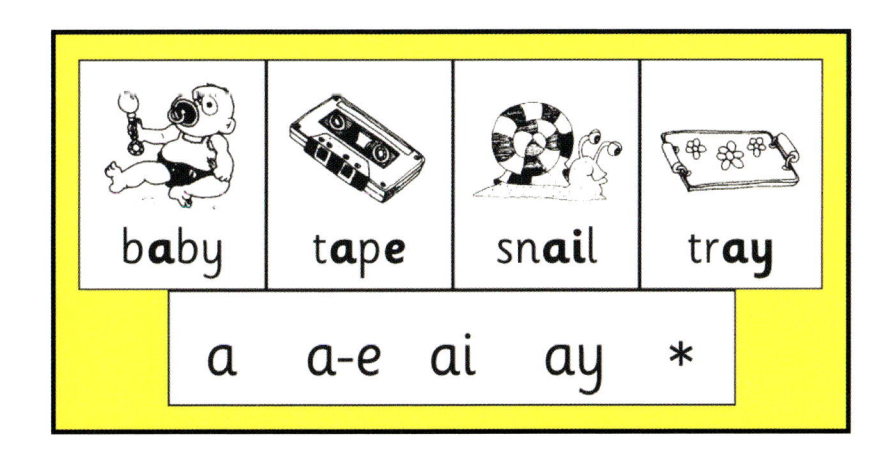

Category
THRASS
TEACHING HANDWRITING READING AND SPELLING SKILLS
FAMILY
SING-A-LONG

baby	tape	snail	tray
a	a-e	ai	ay	*

NOT PHOTOCOPIABLE © 2007 ALARY LTD

Phoneme Symbol = eɪ   Musical Style: Swinging Boogie

are   air

Disco hair

Disco **hair**, I've got disco **hair**.
Can you see my cool disco h**air**?
I'm gonna spell it 'a' 'i' 'r',
'Cause I'm a spelling star
And I am gonna go so far!

So grab three friends,
And dance in a disco **square**. [x 2]

Squ**are** is 'a' and 'r' and 'e'.
Won't you sing along with me?
Spelling words is fun you see. [S]

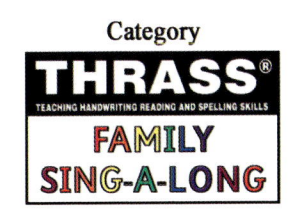

NOT PHOTOCOPIABLE © 2007 ALARY LTD

Phoneme Symbol = eə   Musical Style: 80's Disco

ar a

A great big gorilla

A great big gorilla was driving his c**ar**,
Reminding himself to spell it 'a' 'r'.
He started to cry as he travelled along,
And began to sing this sad little song.

I want a ba ba ba, ba ba **banana**,
Ba ba ba, ba ba ban**a**na.
Ba ba ba, ba ba ban**a**na.
Spell it with one 'a'.

I want a ba ba ba, ba ba **banana**,
Ba ba ba, ba ba ban**a**na.
Ba ba ba, ba ba ban**a**na.
Spell it with one 'a'. [S]

Phoneme Symbol = ɑː   Musical Style: Charleston

e ea

Get outta bed

Early mornin', ain't no snorin',

Get outta **bed** and bake some **bread**.

B**e**d is 'e' and br**ea**d is 'e' 'a'.

Get outta **bed** and bake some **bread**.

Grab your partner, round you go,

Clap your hands and touch your toes.

Grab your partner, round you go,

Stretch up high; now bend down low.   [S] [P1]

Phoneme Symbol = e

Musical Style: Hoedown

ee y e ea

ey

Just me on the beach

Just **me** on the **beach**,
Underneath a **tree**, that's the **key**.
Just **me** on the **beach**,
Underneath a **tree**, that's the **key**.

Dreaming of my **pony** all day long,
Dreaming of my **pony** can't be wrong.

M**e** is spelt with 'e' and b**ea**ch 'e' and 'a',
And tr**ee** is double 'e' and k**ey** 'e' 'y',
And, to spell pon**y**, you just need one 'y'.

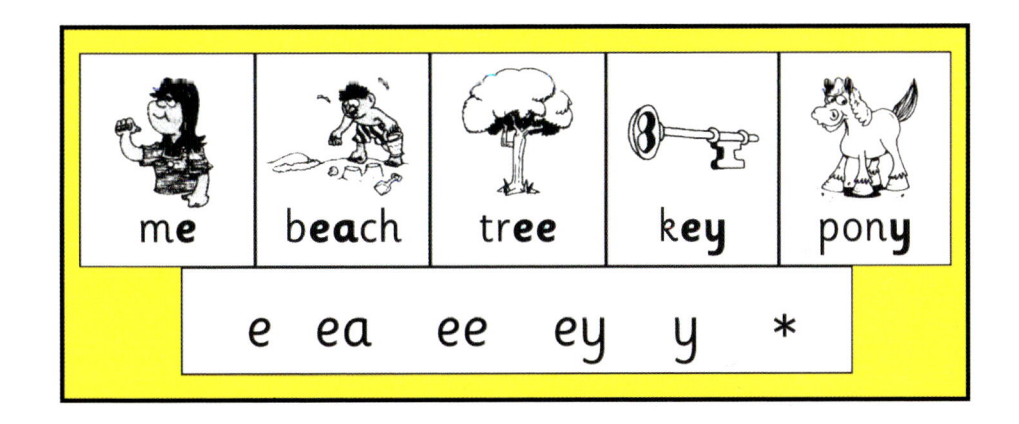

Phoneme Symbol = iː   Musical Style: Hawaiian

eer

ear

The oom pah pah melody

The oom pah pah melody rings in my **ear**,

As through the Black Forest

I'm searching for **deer**.

The oom pah pah melody rings in my **ear**,

As I am out searching for **deer**.

Oom pah pah **ear**, 'e', 'a', 'r',

Oom pah pah d**eer**, 'e', 'e', 'r'.

Oom pah pah **ear**, 'e', 'a', 'r',

Oom pah pah **deer**. [x 2] [P1]

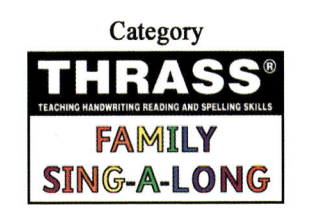

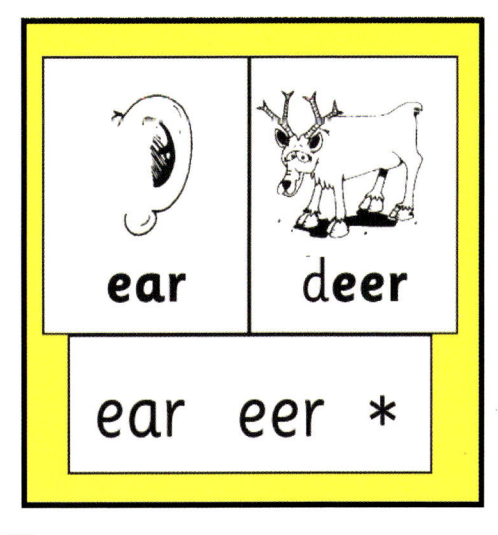

Phoneme Symbol = ɪə   Musical Style: Ober Waltz

or o ure
i
u ar

er e
a

I had a teacher

I had a **teacher**, who had a long collar.
She called the **doctor**, who said he must **measure**.
He said his **zebra** could chew it shorter,
But, oh my gosh, would you believe
It ate the school **garden**?

Now in that **garden** we found a **fossil**,
The **fossil** of a **lion** so we sent it to the **circus**,
And at that **circus** there was a **zebra**,
And, oh my gosh, would you believe
It ate the school **garden**?

Now teach**er** is 'e' 'r', and coll**ar** is 'a' 'r',
And doct**or** is 'o' 'r', and meas**ure** is 'u' 'r' 'e',
And zebr**a** is 'a' and gard**en** is 'e',
And f**o**ssil is 'i', and li**o**n 'o' and circ**u**s is a 'u'.

Wow! Yeehargh!

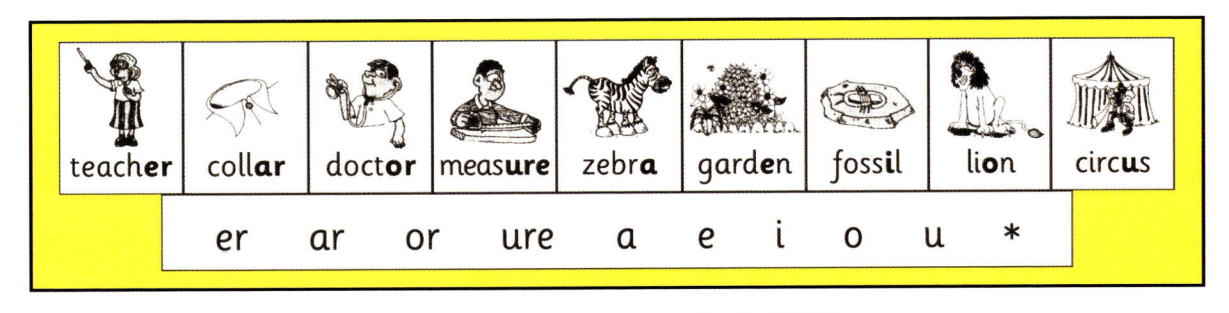

Category: **THRASS** FAMILY SING-A-LONG

NOT PHOTOCOPIABLE © 2007 ALARY LTD

Phoneme Symbol = ə   Musical Style: Bluegrass

er ir or ur

My teddy bear and I

My teddy bear and I, we love to play,
Near the big **fern**, in the garden, every day.
My teddy wears a bright red **shirt**,
And watches while I dig for **worms**.
Then when I'm done, I kiss his soft **fur**,
And say, "It's time to learn".

I say "f**er**n", he says 'e' 'r',
I say "sh**ir**t", he says 'i' 'r',
I say "w**or**m", he says 'o' 'r'.
"And **fur** teddy, who is your best friend?"
And he says, he says, he says, " 'u' 'r' ".

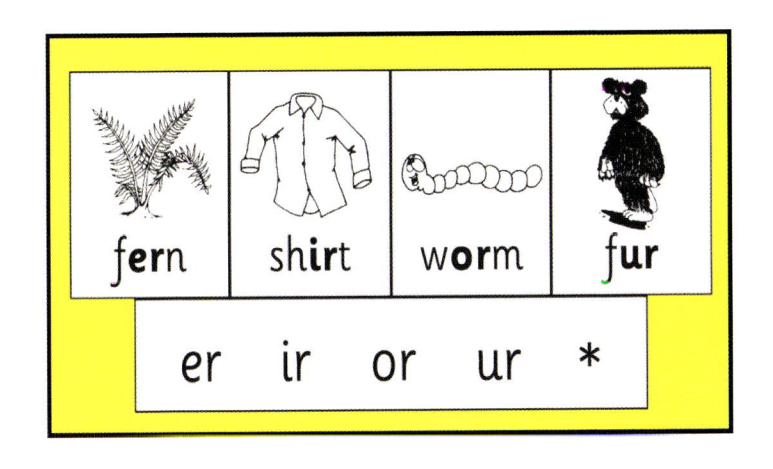

Phoneme Symbol = 3:

Musical Style: Typical 6/8

i   e

Tin Can Man

Tin Can Man flying straight to Mars,

In your **rocket**, past the stars.

Speed of light, see the **tin** man go!

His red **rocket** sure ain't slow.

Even on Mars he spells t**in** with 'i',

And rock**e**t with 'e'.

See it fly, fly, fly.

Even on Mars he spells t**in** with 'i',

And rock**e**t with 'e'.

See it fly, fly, fly. [P1]

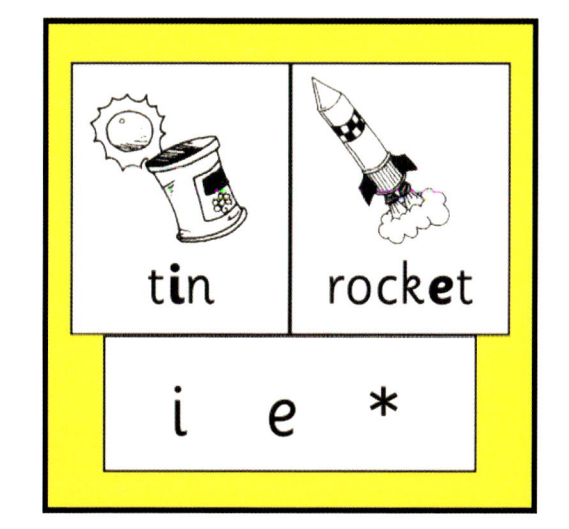

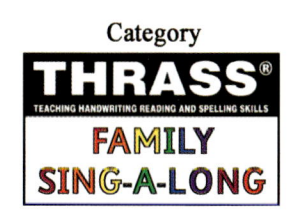

Phoneme Symbol = I   Musical Style: Sci-fi March

i

i-e

igh

y

There is a bright shining tiger

There is a bright shining **tiger**
Painted on my **kite**.
It's so bright it still shines on
When I turn off my **light**.
Tomorrow up into the sky
My **kite** will go up very high,
Higher than a little buzzing **fly**.

T**i**ger is 'i', k**ite** is 'i' 'e',
L**igh**t is 'i' 'g' 'h' and fl**y** is 'y'
T**i**ger is 'i'. [P1+P2]

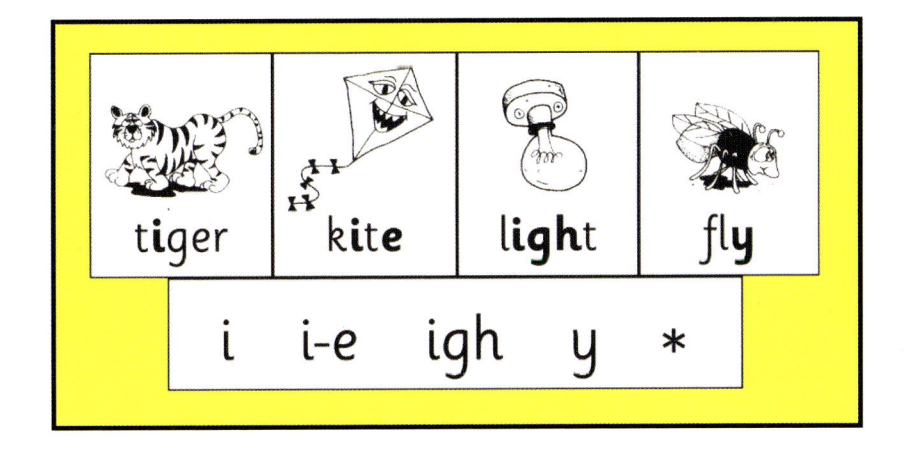

Phoneme Symbol = aɪ   Musical Style: Pentatonic

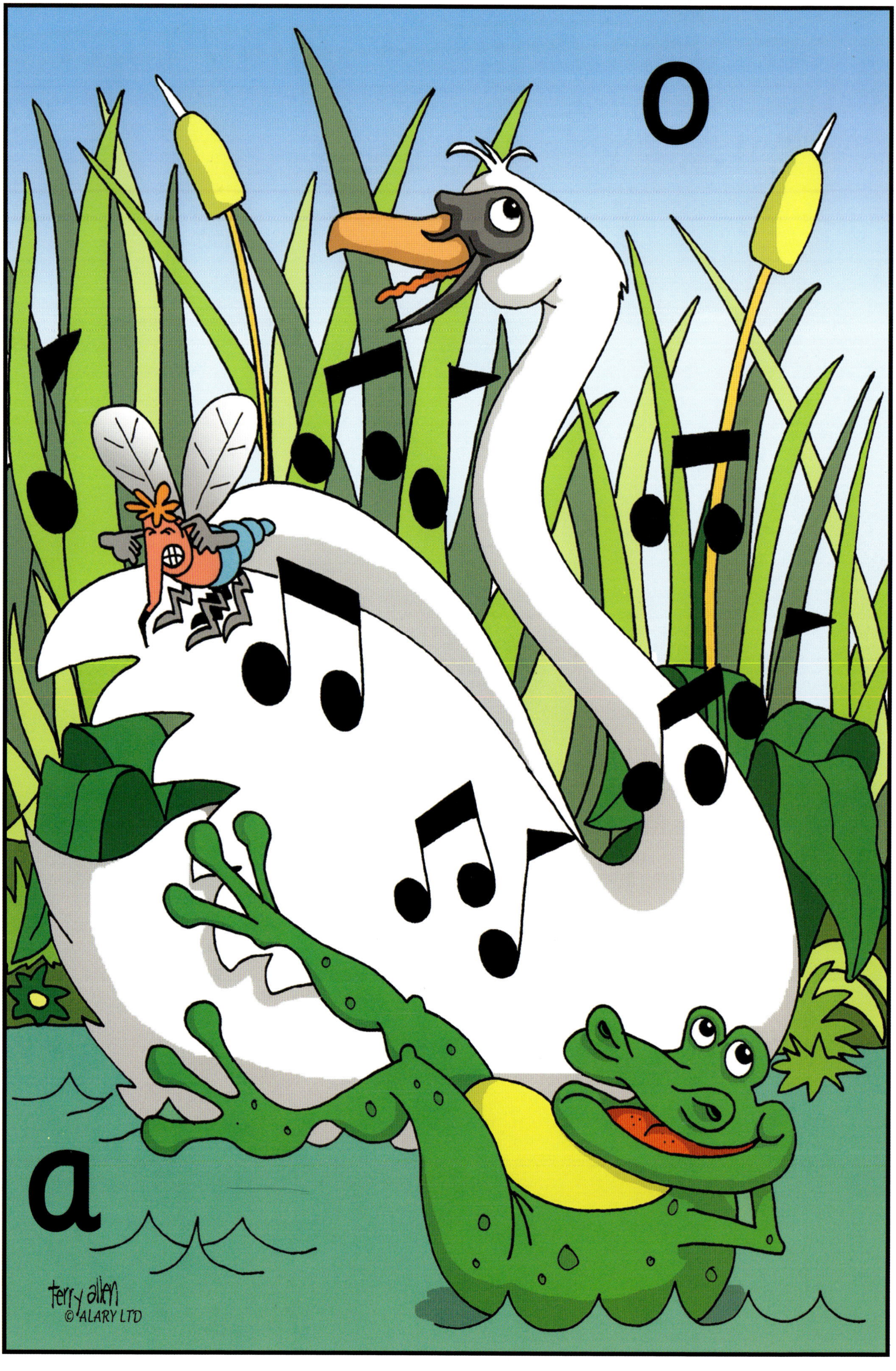
o
a
terry allen
© ALARY LTD

Once upon a time

Once upon a time

There was a **frog** and a **swan**.

They would swim all day

And sing this merry love song.

One, two, three, fr**o**g is 'o'.

One, two, three, sw**a**n is 'a'.

One, two, three, one, two, three.

One. [S]

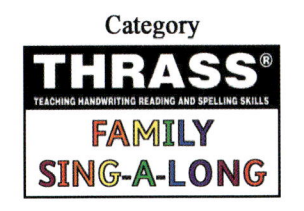

Category
THRASS
TEACHING HANDWRITING READING AND SPELLING SKILLS
FAMILY SING-A-LONG

NOT PHOTOCOPIABLE © 2007 ALARY LTD

Phoneme Symbol = ɒ   Musical Style: Viennese Waltz

oa o-e ow

Eskimos kiss with their nose

Do you know that Eskimos*,
They kiss with their **nose**,
Ride in their **boat**, while singing a **note**,
In the **snow**, the **snow**? [x 2]

Do you know that n**o**se is 'o'?
And b**oa**t is 'o' 'a',
N**o**t**e** is 'o' 'e'.
It's easy you see.
And the sn**ow**, the sn**ow**, is 'o' 'w'.

Category
THRASS
TEACHING HANDWRITING READING AND SPELLING SKILLS
FAMILY
SING-A-LONG

* Eskimo or Inuit? To date, no replacement term for Eskimo inclusive of all Inuit and Yupik people has achieved acceptance across the geographical area inhabited by the Inuit and Yupik peoples.

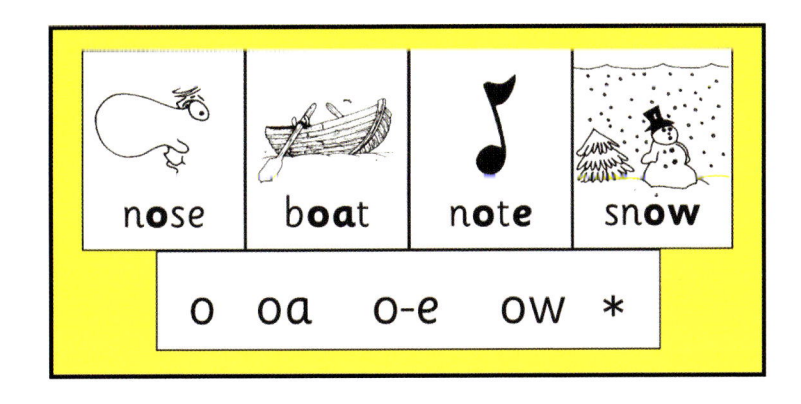

nose	boat	note	snow
o	oa	o-e	ow *

NOT PHOTOCOPIABLE © 2007 ALARY LTD

Phoneme Symbol = əʊ　　　　　　Musical Style: Jazz Ballad

oy oi

TOY SHOP

My coin

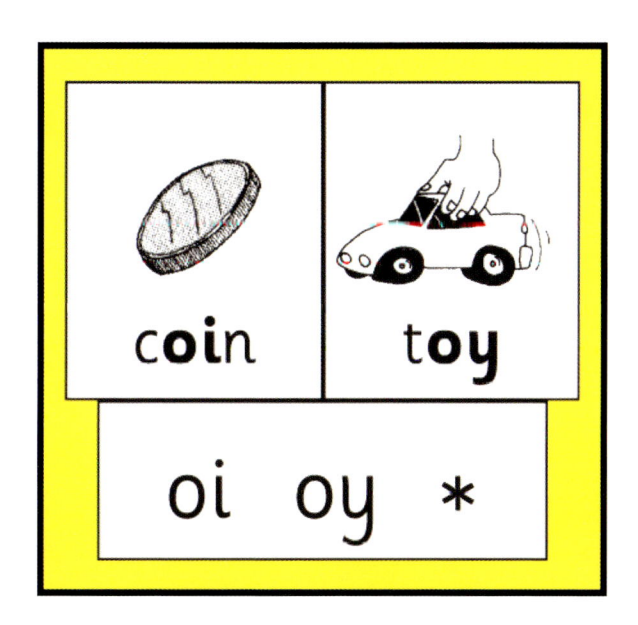

My c**oi**n, 'o' 'i' am so sorry that I lost you,

For now I can't buy a **toy**, 'o' 'y', 'o' 'y'.

Oh why did I lose my **coin**?

My c**oi**n, 'o' 'i' am so sorry that I lost you,

For now I can't buy a t**oy**, 'o' 'y', 'o' 'y',

Oh why did I lose my **coin**?

Phoneme Symbol = ɔɪ   Musical Style: Blues

u oo

I am reading a book

I am reading a **book** about a **bull** fight,

And the matador's cape

Is coloured black and white.

I am reading a **book** about a **bull** fight,

And the matador's cape

Is coloured black and white.

Spell b**oo**k double 'o',

And b**u**ll with one 'u'.

Spell b**oo**k double 'o'

And b**u**ll with one 'u'. [x 2] [P1]

Phoneme Symbol = ʊ Musical Style: Pasodoble

ue
ew
oo

The moon fell out of the sky

The **moon** fell out of the sky
From really way up high.
Can we use a **screw** or **glue**
To make our **moon** brand new? [x 2]

M**oo**n is double 'o',
Scr**ew** is 'e' 'w',
And gl**ue** is 'u' and 'e'.

M**oo**n is double 'o',
Scr**ew** is 'e' 'w',
And gl**ue** is 'u' and 'e'. [S]

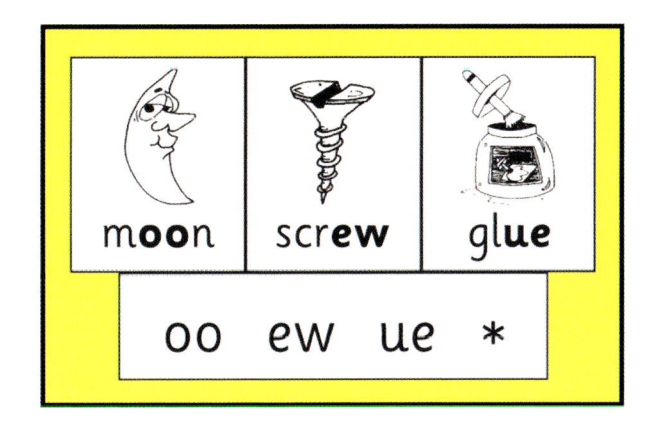

Phoneme Symbol = u: Musical Style: Ragtime

oor

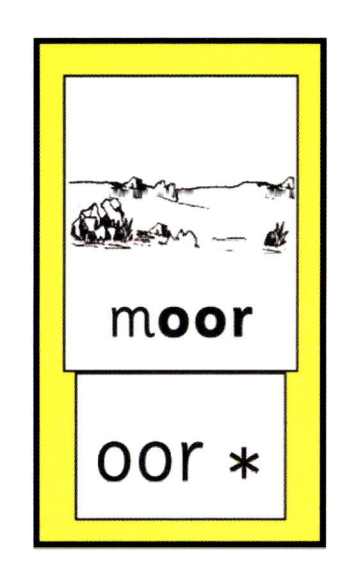

I'm a Scottish dragon

I'm a Scottish dragon and my name's MacFie.

I like to eat shortbread with my tea.

I live in a misty, marshy **moor**.

If you come and visit I will give you a tour.

I'm a Scottish dragon and I like to THRASS.

You may think I'm a lad

But I'm actually a lass.

Visit my **moor**. It is not far,

And if you need to spell m**oor**,

Use 'o' 'o' 'r'.

If you need to spell m**oor**,

Use 'o' 'o' 'r'.

Phoneme Symbol = ʊə   Musical Style: Highland Waltz

or oor
au
aw

a

At six o'clock

At six o'clock my mummy calls me in to eat.
There is a knife and a **fork** at my usual seat.
She puts away my soccer **ball**
And hands me the s**auce**.
The food is yuk.
I really hope there's only one course!
My food's so burnt that I need a s**aw**
To cut through the crust. Look! The centre's raw!
I need to escape before I hurt my jaw.
I wish I could run right out the d**oor**.

Spell f**or**k 'o' 'r' and b**a**ll with 'a',
S**au**ce 'a' 'u'. Look my food is blue!
S**aw** 'a' 'w', d**oor** 'o' 'o' 'r'.
Can I go now please mama?
Please mama?

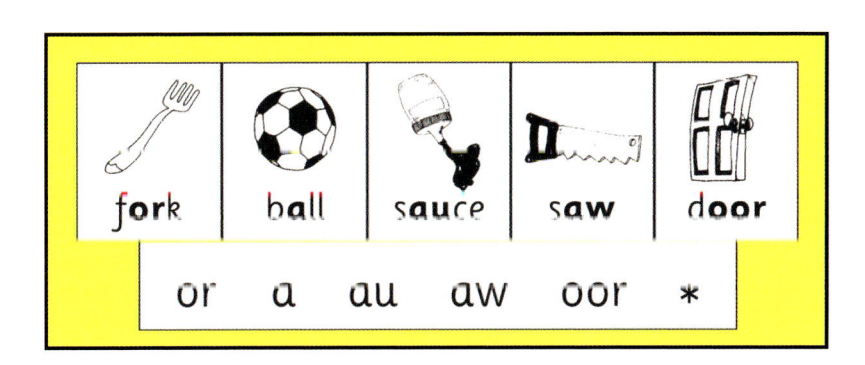

Phoneme Symbol = ɔː

Musical Style: Fun 4/4

ow

ou

Do you know I have a cow?

Do you know I have a **cow**,

A **cow** who lives inside my **house**?

That **cow** loves to sing and dance,

Dance inside my **house**.

C**ow** is spelt with 'o' 'w'.

H**ou**se is spelt with 'o' and 'u'.

C**ow** is spelt with 'o' 'w'.

H**ou**se is spelt 'o' 'u'. [S] [S]

Phoneme Symbol = aʊ   Musical Style: Irish Dance

u o

Plunkett's

Riding along in the bus with 'u'

Riding along in the **bus** with 'u'.
Riding along in the **bus** with 'u'.

With a **glove** on my right hand,
A **glove** on my left hand,
Let's spell gl**o**ve with 'o'.

Singing a song in the **bus** with 'u',
Singing a song in the **bus** with 'u'. [P2]

It's so much fun, spelling b**u**s with 'u'.
It's so much fun, spelling b**u**s with 'u'. [P2]

NOT PHOTOCOPIABLE © 2007 ALARY LTD

Phoneme Symbol = Λ   Musical Style: Orchestra Polka

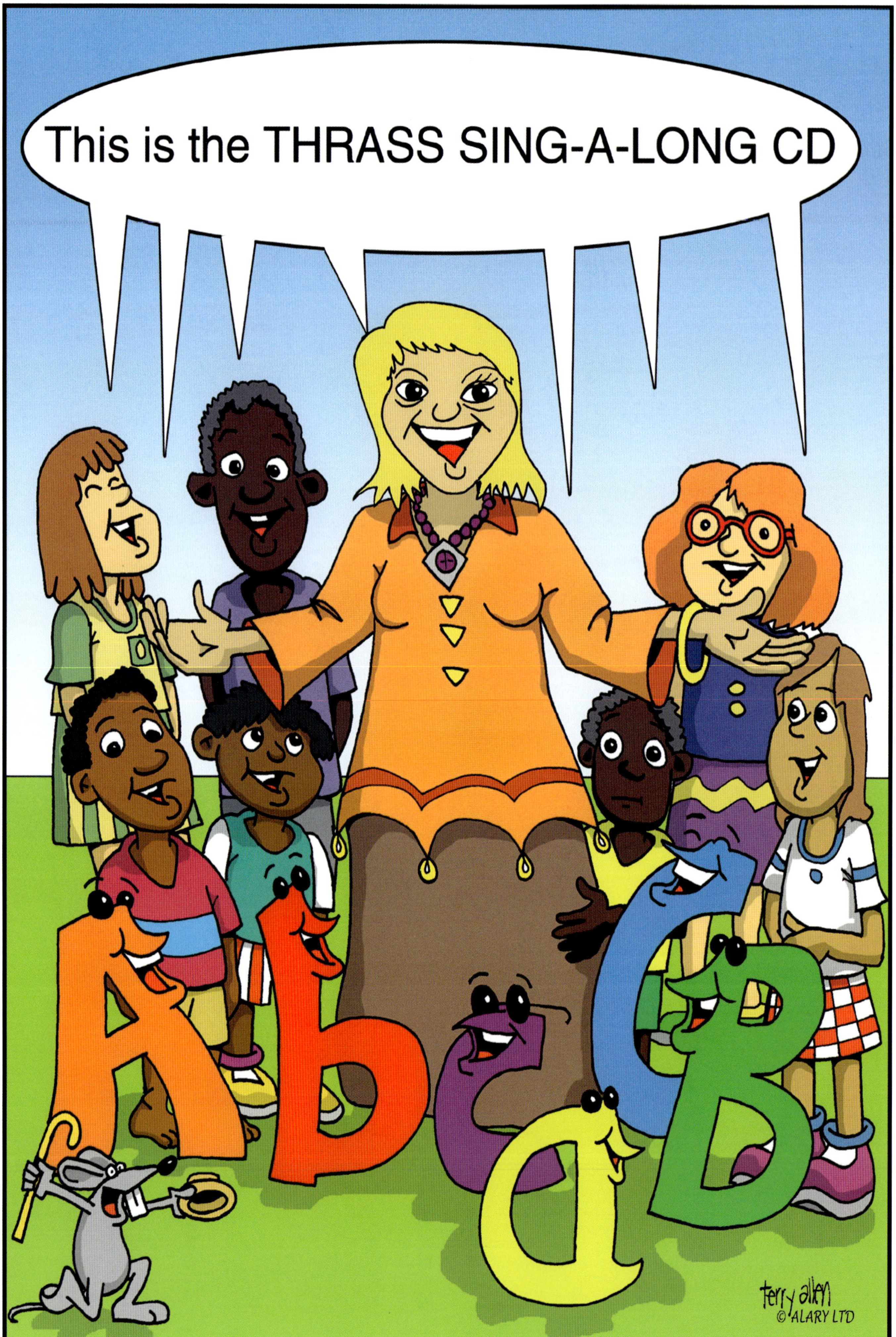
This is the THRASS SING-A-LONG CD
terry allen
© ALARY LTD

THRASS SING-A-LONG CD Song

This is the THRASS SING-A-LONG CD.
Please come along and sing with me.
We'll learn letters like 'a', 'b', 'c'.
A spelling star you will always be.

You'll find that learning letters
Is really lots of fun,
And reading will be easy,
So join me everyone!

This is the THRASS SING-A-LONG CD.
Please come along and sing with me.
We'll learn letters like 'a', 'b', 'c'.
A spelling star you will always be.
A spelling star you will always be!

NOT PHOTOCOPIABLE © 2007 ALARY LTD

Category
THRASS
FAMILY
SING-A-LONG

Musical Style: Fantasy

INFORMATION PAGE

COPYRIGHT NOTICE: ALL RIGHTS RESERVED
No part of this publication may be stored in a retrieval system, reproduced, copied or transmitted in any form or by any means without the prior written permission of the publisher.

THRASS SING-A-LONG BOOK
ISBN 978-1-906295-01-1
First published in 2008 by THRASS (UK) LIMITED

Units 1-3 Tarvin Sands
Barrow Lane, Tarvin
Chester CH3 8JF
England

© 2007 ALARY LTD
Product Code S-01
www.thrass.co.uk
enquiries@thrass.co.uk

THRASS UK LICENSED TERRITORY
THRASS UK is licensed to serve customers in Europe, Africa (including surrounding islands), the Middle East, South America, Central America (including the West Indies), the United States of America and ALSO Central Asia (Pakistan, Afghanistan, Turkmenistan, Uzbekistan and Kazakhstan).

REPEAT 'Buttons'
[P] = Paragraph [S] = Song

SING-A-LONG SPONSORS
for South Africa

School work will never be dull with Pritt. For a lot more inspiring Art, Craft and fun ideas visit www.prittworld.com
Tollfree 0800 13 81 81

An initiative with a vision to increase literacy in South Africa through the improved teaching and learning of English. The project provides a platform to celebrate South Africa's eleven national languages through free interactive and printable calendar charts. SMS 32828*, www.talktogether.co.za, POST TO: Absa Foundation, P O Box 7735, Johannesburg 2000. *SMS costs R1.

PUBLIC PERFORMANCES
A public performance is an infringement of copyright. Performance of the songs at home or before an audience of teachers and pupils/students at an educational establishment is permissible. Performance of the songs in concerts for parents is also permissible, provided that a royalty is paid in the form of a discretionary donation to a charity and THRASS UK are informed of the amount of the donation and the name of the charity. The making of a recording by a parent, teacher or other person is an infringement of copyright. Warnings should be given before the start of performances and concerts. If other individuals, groups or organisations wish to perform the songs, a licence must be obtained from ALARY LTD (c/o THRASS UK).

SING-A-LONG RESOURCES www.thrass.co.uk/resources.htm
S-01 SING-A-LONG BOOK ISBN 978-1-906295-01-1
S-02 SING-A-LONG CD ISBN 978-1-906295-02-8
S-03 SING-A-LONG INTERACTIVE BOOK ISBN 978-1-906295-03-5
S-04 SING-A-LONG COLOURING BOOK ISBN 978-1-906295-04-2
S-05 MOVE-A-LONG WITH SING-A-LONG DVD ISBN 978-1-906295-05-9
S-06 SING-A-LONG SHEET MUSIC BOOK ISBN 978-1-906295-06-6

OTHER ASSOCIATED THRASS RESOURCES
T-03 THRASS PICTURECHART Desk Size and/or Class Size T-02
T-51 THRASS RAPS AND SEQUENCES CD
T-06 THRASS OVERWRITE CHART

ADULTS LEARNING ENGLISH:
The SING-A-LONG resources are also useful for agencies that help adults to learn English, especially if the adults are parents that want to help their own children.

FORMAL & INFORMAL LANGUAGE IN THE SING-A-LONG SONGS
Where appropriate, words of informal language (such as the word 'outta' in the 'Get outta bed' Hoedown) have been used to reinforce a musical style. It is assumed that the SING-A-LONG resources will not be the only literacy materials to be used in school and at home, and that teachers and parents will encourage their children to speak, hear, read and spell the formal language alternatives. When speaking with others, reading books and listening to radio and/or television, children are exposed to both formal and informal language and they usually learn, from experiences in school and at home, when and where to use the appropriate words and spellings.

THANKS to....
MY family, especially my husband and children, for their love and support. JP
WOUNDED BUFFALO Recording Studio, The Media Mill, Milpark, Johannesburg. www.woundedbuffalo.co.za
LAPDUST Audio Mastering, Parklands, Johannesburg. www.lapdust.com
AB - our helpful Wordsmith.
YAMAHA - all the music has been produced on Tyros2 - the best digital keyboard ever!

MOVE-A-LONG WITH SING-A-LONG WORKSHOPS
These one-day workshops are for teachers and/or parents to have fun while gaining group experience of singing and performing the actions to a good range of tracks on the double CD. The workshops include small and large group work and watching and discussing recorded performances of schoolchildren.

COLOUR FILTERS FOR OFFENSIVE LIGHT WAVES
If one or more of your learners are sensitive to specific wavelengths of light (research pioneered by our good friend Helen Irlen, Long Beach, California) it may be that colour filters (to alter the amount of the problem shade of colour entering the eye) need to be worn or placed over the printed page/screen. Check it out - www.irlen.com